ANCIENT ROME

SIMON JAMES

TED SMART

Acknowledgements

The publishers would like to thank Bill Le Fever, who illustrated the see-through
pages and jacket; and the organizations which have
given their permission to reproduce the following pictures:

Ronald Sheridan/Ancient Art & Architecture Collection: 4 (top left), 4 (bottom left), 10,
18 (top left), 20, 30 (top left), 30 (top right), 32 (bottom), 40
British Museum: 13 (bottom right)
Peter Clayton: 16, 22 (top left)
C. M. Dixon: 38 (right)
Werner Forman Archive: 30 (bottom), 32 (top left), 34 (top left), 34 (bottom)
Sonia Halliday Photographs: 22 (bottom), 37, 45
Robert Harding Picture Library: 26 (Sheila Terry)
Michael Holford: 7, 14 (top right), 21, 26, 28 (top left), 36, 38 (left), 44
Simon James: 39 (bottom)
Magnum: 6, 14 (top left)
Museum of London: 24
Scala: 18 (bottom left)
Service Photographique de la Reunion des Musées Nationaux: 28 (bottom)

Illustrators:
Philip Hood (Young Artists)**:** 6-7, 8, 9, 10, 11, 12-13, 14, 15, 16, 18-19, 22-23, 24, 26-27, 29,
34-35, 36, 37, 39, 40 (top right), 43, 44
Bill Le Fever: 17, 25, 33, 41
Nigel Longden: 20, 21, 42, 46-47
Kevin Madison: 4-5, 26 (bottom left), 40 (bottom left)
Shirley Mallinson: 31

Hamlyn Children's Books:
Editor: Andrew Farrow
Series Designer: Nick Leggett
Picture Research: Ann Pestell
Production Controller: Linda Spillane

This edition first published in 1995 for The Book People,
Guardian House, Borough Road, Godalming, Surrey GU7 2AE by
Hamlyn Children's Books, an imprint of Reed Children's Books,
Michelin House, 81 Fulham Road, London SW3 6RB,
and Auckland, Melbourne, Singapore and Toronto.

ISBN 1-856-13874-7

British Library Cataloguing-in-Publication Data.
A catalogue record for this book is available from the British Library.

Books printed and bound in Belgium

CONTENTS

THE BIRTH OF ROME

A cameo (consisting of a gem carved from a stone with coloured layers) showing Augustus, the first Emperor of Rome. Originally he wore the victor's laurel-leaf crown: the jewels were added in later times.

In the seventh century BC, Rome was a small, rustic Italian town on the banks of the River Tiber. By the first century AD, it had grown into a vast metropolis of over a million people, and it ruled most of the world known to the Romans.

FROM LITTLE ACORNS...

Rome's rise to world power was sudden. At first it had grown only very slowly, and there was nothing obviously special about it - there were many such independent city states in the Mediterranean at the time. About 509 BC, the last king was driven out and Rome became a republic. The city gradually dominated its Latin-speaking neighbours, and clashed with the powerful Etruscan cities and the warlike peoples of the central Italian mountains. It also came into contact with the rich and cultured Greek cities of the South. Rome was greatly impressed by Greek civilization and copied many aspects of it.

BEGINNINGS OF EMPIRE

The wolf and twins, symbol of the origins of Rome. It was said that the sons of the war-god Mars, Romulus and Remus, were suckled by a she-wolf. Romulus is supposed to have founded Rome in 753 BC.

Despite setbacks, by the 260s BC Rome was the strongest state in Italy. Trouble in Sicily drew Rome into a series of wars, called the Punic Wars, against the North African sea-power of Carthage, an immensely rich trading city founded by the Phoenicians. The Punic Wars involved vast armies and fleets and caused terrible destruction. Italy was ravaged by Hannibal, the famous Carthaginian general, who led his army, with elephants, over the Alps. He smashed several Roman armies. The legions attacked the Carthaginian lands and campaigned overseas for the first time, in Spain and Africa. Carthage was finally defeated and destroyed in 146 BC.

SUPERPOWER

The furnace of the Punic Wars forged Rome into a world power. It learned how to control and fight with large armies. It acquired new territories which became the first provinces of the Empire. Also, the warfare in Southern Italy drew Rome into the complex politics of the Greek world, which stretched to Syria and beyond. As a result, Rome clashed with the big Greek-ruled kingdoms in Macedonia and Western Asia. By 160 BC these Westerners, who seemed uncouth to the proud Greeks, dominated the whole of the Mediterranean, and Greek embassies streamed to Rome for judgements in the quarrels and disputes between the Greek states.

COLLAPSE OF THE REPUBLIC

In just a century, then, from about 260 to 160 BC, Rome became mistress of the Mediterranean, changing the balance of power in the ancient world. In the process Rome changed very much itself. Conquests brought vast wealth to its leaders. On the other hand, millions of prisoners of war began to flood into Italy as slaves, and the conquered states were ill-governed and impoverished. Worse, the Roman armies proved to be more loyal to their generals than to their country, and warlords such as Julius Caesar fought each other for power. The old Republic dissolved into civil wars which raged across the Empire for much of the last century BC.

THE IMPERIAL PEACE

Finally, peace was restored and a new system of government was established by Augustus, the first Emperor (who reigned from 27 BC to AD 14). The provinces were better treated and, above all, peace was enforced throughout the Empire. Under the Emperors who followed Augustus, during the first and second centuries AD, the whole Mediterranean world was at peace and under a single government for the only time in its history. Trade flourished, and people came to share a common way of life and common languages, Greek or Latin. This, the early Empire, was the golden age of Roman civilization, and is the period which forms the main subject of this book.

At the height of its power in the second century AD, the Roman Empire spanned the whole of the Mediterranean world, covering lands now occupied by about 30 modern countries, ranging from Morocco to the Scottish borders and to Rumania, Egypt and Syria.

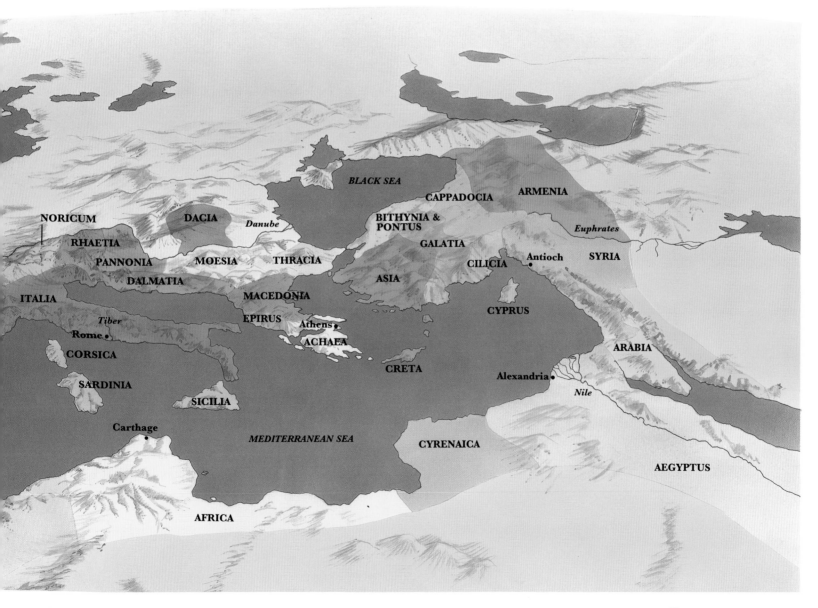

THE COUNTRYSIDE

A bronze model of a cockerel, from France. The Romans kept poultry for both meat and eggs.

A villa in the Italian countryside, standing on an arched platform overlooking its farming lands. Oxen are pulling a plough in the grain-fields. Meanwhile, slaves and farm labourers are picking the fruit from olive trees to take to the villa, where great stone presses will squeeze out the oil ready for shipment to the towns.

The Roman Empire is famous for its magnificent cities, of which Rome itself was the biggest. Yet Rome relied mostly on the produce of the countryside for its wealth and everyday needs.

FARMING

Most of the people of the Empire lived in the country and worked on the land. In such a vast area as the Empire there were many different types of farming, according to the climate and type of countryside. The heartlands of the Empire, on the warm shores of the Mediterranean Sea, grew wheat and other cereals, but the most prized crops were grapes for making wine and olives for eating or for making olive oil. Then - as now - olive oil was essential for Mediterranean cooking. It was also used for lamps, and even for cleaning the body.

Most of the animals bred on farms today were also kept by Roman farmers, especially pigs, cattle and sheep. There were big cattle ranches in Italy, and sheep in mountainous areas too steep to plough.

'Lands adjoining my property are for sale. Many things in them tempt me... the property is fertile, rich, and well supplied with water, and consists of meadows, vineyards, and woods that produce an income from timber...'

From a letter by Pliny

PRODUCE OF THE PROVINCES

Different areas became famous for certain agricultural products. For example, Egypt and North Africa produced the grain that fed the people of the city of Rome, Italy made famous wines and Spain produced excellent olive oil. Britain, partly conquered in AD 43, was too cold to produce olives, but the woollen goods and beer from there seem to have had a good reputation.

On rivers such as the Nile, and in numerous small villages around the coasts, fishing was an important part of the local economy, though keeping the catch fresh was a problem in hot regions.

WOOD AND WOODLANDS

Forests and woods were very important to the Empire, just as they are to us today. Large trees were felled for building, and smaller trees were regularly cut and allowed to re-grow, to provide renewable supplies of fuel for cooking and for heating homes and the great bath-houses.

FIELDS

In parts of Italy the roads and fields of the modern landscape still follow the lines of the vast chequerboard pattern laid out by Roman surveyors, who distributed the land to the farmers fairly, in measured rectangular plots. However, over most of the Empire, fields and paddocks were less regular.

Of course, the Romans did much less environmental damage than we do - there were fewer people - but over-grazing and soil exhaustion were problems in some areas.

VILLAGES AND VILLAS

Across the land were settlements, where the farming communities lived. These were villages and hamlets, small farmsteads and, especially in Italy, splendid villas.

Above is a detail of a large floor-mosaic, showing the exotic landscape of Egypt, always a favourite subject for Romans. The fertile farmlands of Egypt yielded an enormous amount of grain and gold as taxes, so the Emperors kept it under their personal control.

The wealthy spent much of their time conducting business in town, either in trade or politics. Yet owning farmland was thought to be the only proper way for noble Romans to make a living. There was a romantic yearning amongst the wealthy for the peace and beauty of a country estate, away from the hurly-burly of city life, where they could relax and indulge in rural pleasures like hunting and picnicking.

A LIFE OF LUXURY

However, they did not want to leave the luxuries of their town houses behind, so they built splendid country houses, called villas, with all the comforts of town life - not least of which was a bath-house.

The estates attached to these beautiful houses were largely run by slaves, whose real lives were grindingly hard and far removed from the romantic view of some of the rich city people.

Although we think first of the great splendours of the Empire, none of these could have existed without the food and wealth produced by the farming folk.

The groma was a surveying device. It was used for laying out straight lines and right-angles by sighting along the weighted strings.

MASTERS AND SLAVES

The people of Rome, and of the many other societies in the Empire, in some ways seem strange to us today. For example, people were not assumed to be equal, even in the eyes of the law. Almost everyone was accustomed to the existence of slavery, which was an important part of Roman life. Few thought that it was wrong. Also, the Empire was very much a man's world, in which women and girls had only limited rights under the law.

SLAVES AND FREEDMEN

In Italy, millions of slaves worked on the estates of the rich, and wealthier households all had servants who were either slaves or ex-slaves. Within this system, slaves could be freed, or they could buy their freedom. For example, many house-slaves, especially educated Greeks bought as tutors for the children, were treated as friends, and were often freed. As 'freedmen' they continued to serve their former masters.

At least some slaves in wealthy households were treated as part of the family as we would understand it. There were cases of much-loved slaves being not only freed, but adopted as heirs to estates, or even marrying a former master.

CITIZENS AND PROVINCIALS

Even among the wealthy people of the Empire there were important distinctions. Most people who were not slaves were citizens of their particular city, places such as Venta Belgarum (Winchester) in Britain, Cyrene in North Africa or Damascus in Syria. People who were citizens of Rome had special privileges.

One of the remarkable things about Rome was that it was generous in granting Roman citizenship to anyone considered worthy, wherever they came from. For example, soldiers from the provinces who served for 20 years or more were made Roman citizens, as were magistrates of other cities. One famous Roman citizen was St Paul, a Greek-speaking Jewish doctor from Turkey!

In this strange ceremony, slaves are being freed by being touched by a rod called a vindicta. *They are wearing the Cap of Liberty, which has been used as a symbol of freedom down to modern times.*

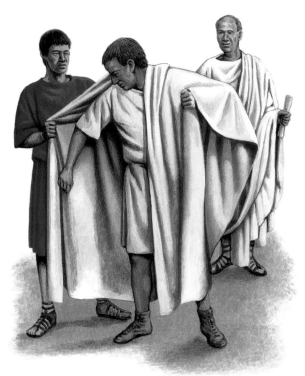

THE IMPERIAL HOUSEHOLD

The most powerful patron of all was the Emperor, on whose favour depended all of the important governorships and army commands of the Empire, as well as rich commissions for architects, artists and a host of other people. To get such favours it was necessary to win the attention of the Emperor. Audiences with the ruler of Rome were controlled by his secretaries, who were therefore very powerful and rich. In the early Empire these men were freedmen of the Emperor, ex-slaves who were more powerful even than the senators, who had to give favours to the secretaries if they wanted to reach the Emperor!

Senators were not supposed to involve themselves in trade. In fact they did so through their own clients, especially their freedmen, who ran businesses, such as this marble-quarry, for their patrons.

A slave helping his master to put on his toga, *the heavy white gown which was the mark of a Roman citizen. Senators and boys had* togas *with a purple edge. The* toga *was heavy, uncomfortable and hard to keep clean.*

PATRONS AND CLIENTS

The magistrates who ruled the city states of the Empire, including Rome, were elected by the votes of the male citizens. This does not mean it was a democracy as we understand it today - for instance, neither slaves nor women were allowed to vote.

In the Roman world, important people, known as patrons, had dependants whom they looked after. The dependants were called clients. Clients expected their patrons to help them out when they were in trouble, or to assist them in their careers. Patrons, especially those wealthy enough to seek office as magistrates or other top jobs, expected their clients to vote for them.

This system often worked quite well, but could be taken to dangerous extremes. For example, in the later years of the Republic, powerful men such as Julius Caesar had entire armies which regarded their general as a patron who would look after them. This fuelled the civil wars which destroyed the old Republic. However, the system of seeking favours from the great, and helping people you thought to be worthy, was how the Roman world continued to work.

One of the best preserved of all Roman buildings is this beautiful temple, the maison carrée *in Nimes, France. It shows the grandeur and richness of Roman public buildings.*

Towns and cities were the building blocks of the Roman Empire. There were thousands of them, some of them very small, others very great indeed, such as Rome itself, Alexandria in Egypt, or Antioch in Syria.

BUILDING THE CITIES

Many of the cities existed before the rise of the Empire. Some were already hundreds or even thousands of years old. Others had been founded by the Greeks who settled in much of the Mediterranean and surrounding lands. In areas such as Gaul (France) and in Britain, there were no cities as the Greeks and Romans knew them: Gauls and Britons had not felt much need to build even small towns. The Romans encouraged them to build towns and cities in the Roman style.

A MOSAIC OF CITY-STATES

Most cities were like little states, controlling the lands around them. They were governed by councils of important local people, most of whom were landowners. Magistrates (mayors, judges and city officials) were elected from the council members by the citizens. These magistrates enforced the laws, kept the streets and public buildings in good repair and collected taxes for the city and the Roman government.

There were frequent elections: 'posters' promoting candidates have been found painted on the walls of Pompeii.

THE SHAPE OF A TOWN

Towns were made up of networks of streets and blocks. These blocks, called *insulae*, contained houses, shops, workshops and bars. Some - often in the middle of the town - were reserved for splendid public buildings.

At the centre of the town there was usually a forum, or market place, where people assembled to conduct business and gossip. Next to the forum was the basilica or town hall. The forum often contained the most important of the temples in the town, dedicated to the old Roman gods. Other temples around the town were dedicated to a variety of gods, just as today in European cities there are many churches dedicated to various saints, and other places of worship such as mosques and synagogues. Bath-houses were another type of building important in the lives of the town-dwellers.

Most Roman towns were smaller than modern cities, with populations ranging from just a few thousand people to perhaps 20-30,000. Only the great trading cities and capitals of the Empire were bigger than this: Rome itself was home to a million people or more.

Farmers and estate managers inspect cattle and horses at the open market next to the forum. Most smaller towns had few public buildings, but were usually thriving market centres, or were important because they often had a relay station for the Roman government postal service and an inn.

THEATRES AND AMPHITHEATRES

Roman towns are famous for their places of entertainment, which were often decorated as lavishly as the forum and the temples. The Romans loved chariot races, and larger towns had race-tracks, often outside the walls. The Romans also adopted the idea of building theatres in stone from the Greeks. These great D-shaped buildings were surpassed in size only by amphitheatres, the huge oval arenas where gladiators and animals fought in bloody combats.

CITY LIMITS

Around the city or town was a holy boundary, marked out by a sacred plough when the city was founded. Most had fine walls and towers to mark these limits, although in the Roman Peace these, like the splendid public buildings within, were often mainly for decoration, and to show how rich and cultured the town was. People were very proud of their cities and also tried to out-do any neighbouring towns in the lavishness of the buildings they erected.

Outside the gates, the traveller would see cemeteries along the roads, for it was against the law to bury the dead inside the sacred boundary.

AQUEDUCTS AND SEWERS

The Romans built complicated water supply systems, which brought fresh water from distant springs along special channels called aqueducts. Rome itself had 11 aqueducts carrying water into the city. Private houses had their own water supply, but apartment dwellers had to get their water from a communal tap at street level. Many cities had drains to carry away rainwater and sewage, but the streets were still dirty and smelly.

The Romans were great engineers. They built vast structures, such as this aqueduct which today still stands in the south of France. The huge stones were winched into place by simple muscle-power, with the aid of pulleys and cranes.

11

BUSINESS AND GOVERNMENT

Part of the forum at Rome itself, which was much bigger and grander than any other. It had special market halls and many temples built by the Emperors, as well as the house of the senate. Around the market place are (from left to right) the Aemilian hall, the temple of the Emperor Antoninus, and the temple of Venus and Rome (with the Colosseum behind). The temple of Julius Caesar stands next to the arch of Augustus, and then on the right is the temple of the Heavenly Twins and, finally, the Julian hall. The palace of the Emperor is on the hill on the right.

The city was the heart of Roman life, and the forum was the heart of the city. All important towns had a forum: it was an area for markets and for public assemblies, and it was where much of the town's government and the business of its people were carried out.

THE FORUM

In many cities the forum was a great plaza, paved with good stone and surrounded by a portico of columns. Huge sums of money were often spent on such architectural features by wealthy citizens as a gift to the city, and for their own glory. Such donations might be honoured by the placing of the men's statues in the forum itself. There might be many such statues around the forum, of gods, emperors and great men.

There were permanent shops around the forum. On market days, traders and farmers came to town, to set up stalls and to sell and haggle with shoppers.

THE BASILICA

On one side of the forum would be found the city hall, called the basilica, which usually had a roof supported by rows of columns. Inside you would expect to see a statue of the Emperor, and the tribunal where judges sat to consider legal cases. Adjacent to the basilica would be the *curia*, where councillors met to pass local laws and to discuss the collection of taxes.

MAGISTRATES

Roman towns were usually governed by two magistrates, called *duoviri*. They were like mayors and held office for a year.

In Rome the two chief magistrates for the year were known as consuls. They were usually experienced senators. During the early Republic they led the legions in war. Later, from the time of Augustus, the army came under the Emperor's command, but consulships remained prestigious because Rome was a vast city to govern.

TEMPLES

One end of a town's forum was usually dominated by a large temple, dedicated to the gods Jupiter, Juno and Minerva. The townsfolk were expected to make sacrifices to the Roman gods and also venerate the town's own particular guardian deity. For example, Greek cities worshipped the Tyche, or goddess of fortune, of their town.

THE FORUM AT ROME

The forum in Rome was particularly ancient and stood surrounded by famous public buildings. It was overlooked by the lofty Temple of Jupiter on the Capitoline hill, and the great imperial palace on the Palatine. At the heart of the forum was the senate house and the *rostra*, or platform, from which politicians addressed the people. There were many other religious buildings in the forum, such as the Temple of Saturn, the Temple of Julius Caesar (who was declared a god after his death) and the residence of the Vestal Virgins, the ancient order of priestesses.

Nearby there were a number of large and impressive new fora, built by the Emperors to give even more market space and grandeur to the centre of the Empire.

The senate was something like a parliament, although it was not elected. It consisted of very wealthy Roman nobles who had been magistrates. The senate heard debates and made laws.

As senior Roman magistrates had the power to punish and to condemn people to death, they had ceremonial attendants, called lictors. The lictors carried a bundle of rods around an axe to symbolize their power.

THE FAMILY

Roman children played many familiar-looking games, such as pick-a-back and marbles. Boys often played games which involved throwing walnuts, like the French game of boule.

Traditionally, a Roman family (including wife, children and servants) were all under the authority of the father of the household, the *paterfamilias*. Originally he had power of life and death over them all; in practice, this was no longer the case during the Empire.

ROMAN CHILDREN

When children were born, they were laid at the feet of the father. If he accepted the infant into the family, he would pick it up. But many poor families simply could not feed additional mouths, and babies were often 'exposed' - left outside to die or be picked up by compassionate strangers.

Many children were born slaves and were expected to work as soon as they were old enough, perhaps at 6 or 7 years old. Even the children of ordinary free families were unlikely to get schooling; they, too would help their parents at work as soon as they were old enough to do chores.

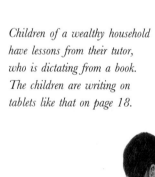

Children of a wealthy household have lessons from their tutor, who is dictating from a book. The children are writing on tablets like that on page 18.

Most children's toys were made of wood and other materials which rotted away long ago, and so few toys survive today. This little wheeled horse from Roman times was preserved by the dry climate of Egypt.

FUN AND GAMES

Even poor children probably found some time for play. We know something of their games from writings and pictures. These show children playing with hoops, pick-a-back fighting, and playing a game like marbles with walnuts, although marbles made of glass were used, too. Ball-games and board-games were also played, as was 'knucklebones', which is similar to dice. Children sometimes had pets - dogs or birds were quite common - and rich ones had expensive toys such as goat-drawn chariots.

14

GOING TO SCHOOL

The privileged few were educated in reading, writing and other basics. They were taught by their father, or by a hired tutor, who was usually a Greek slave.

At school, children learned arithmetic and to read and write Latin and Greek, the two main languages of the Empire. They would soon be learning the works of famous writers and poets, such as Homer and Virgil. These had to be learned by heart; and mistakes and misbehaviour were punished by savage beatings. Many children did not enjoy going to school!

GIRLS AND WOMEN

Girls were given only a basic education, after which it was expected that they would learn domestic skills and house-keeping from their mothers, until they were old enough to marry.

Married women had hard lives, not least because of the dangers of child-birth. In addition to keeping house and raising children, many women had to help their husbands at work as well.

Women also had limited legal rights. When they married, they and their property came under the control of their husbands. However, during the Empire it became possible for women whose husbands died to regain control of their own property, so it is not surprising that widows were reluctant to marry again and lose their independence!

BOYS AND MEN

While their sisters learned to be wives and mothers, teenage boys from rich families went on to learn the skills they would need later in life, such as how to speak to a crowd, or argue a case in a law-court.

Fathers would help their sons start careers in business, law or politics. They arranged introductions to important men who might give them good positions in their chosen career. This use of influence was quite normal in the Roman world.

Roman mansions could be very comfortable. The wealthy led pampered lives with servants to look after all their needs. Here a rich woman is preparing for the day, as her maid dresses her hair. Wall-paintings, elaborate beds and other furnishings like these have been found at Pompeii, and are shown in Roman paintings and sculptures.

15

MANSIONS AND SLUMS

A lar, *a guardian spirit of the household. Roman homes had a small shrine where such figures were kept and sacrificed to.*

This is the sort of place where most Roman town dwellers really lived. Dirty and dangerous narrow streets, and crumbling buildings, were a far cry from the luxury of the rich.

Roman town houses came in all shapes and sizes, from badly-built hovels to lofty blocks of flats and rambling old mansions. Only wealthy Romans could afford to live in a private house, or *domus*, and even fewer could afford a villa, a country house, as well.

PLAN OF A TOWN HOUSE

The traditional Roman house was laid out around a central hall called an *atrium*, with a small yard or, in later times, a big garden, at the back. City blocks were usually made up of several such houses, perhaps with some smaller dwellings and shops between. Some houses had a room on either side of the front door, closed off from the house and opening onto the street. These were rented out as shops.

At Pompeii and other towns, it is possible to see how some houses grew as their owners prospered. They bought the adjacent properties and knocked doorways through to make even larger houses.

'For men of rank, houses should be built with lofty entrance courts in princely style, most spacious *atria* and colonnades, broad groves and walks appropriate to their dignity, and in addition, libraries and porticoes, finished in a style like that of great public buildings...'

— *The architect Vitruvius* —

THE SERVANTS' WORLD

Hidden away from the grander rooms of town houses were the working areas, such as the kitchens and stores. The biggest houses might have their own baths and, especially in the northern provinces, some other rooms had underfloor heating. All the fires to heat these had to be kept stoked up, a hot and dirty job. There were also living quarters for the large numbers of slaves and servants needed by a great household, including cooks, a baker, stewards, maids, and secretaries. There would also be a porter at the front door, with a large guard-dog to see off unwelcome visitors.

HOUSES OF THE POOR

In the big towns, such as Rome, most people lived in poor housing, sometimes in tall blocks of flats which had no water supplies or kitchens. Food, drink and everything else had to be carried up the stairs, and rubbish and sewage carried down - or thrown out of the window. There were often fires, the worst of which was the Great Fire of Rome in AD 64, in which most of the city was destroyed. The Emperors put a 20-metre limit on the height of blocks, and Rome even had a fire brigade, but it made little difference to reducing damage.

The streets of the cities were noisy, dirty and dangerous, with workshops belching fumes, wagons trundling by and tradesmen shouting for business. Crime was common, so it is not surprising that the houses of the great have few outside windows and doors.

A TOWN HOUSE

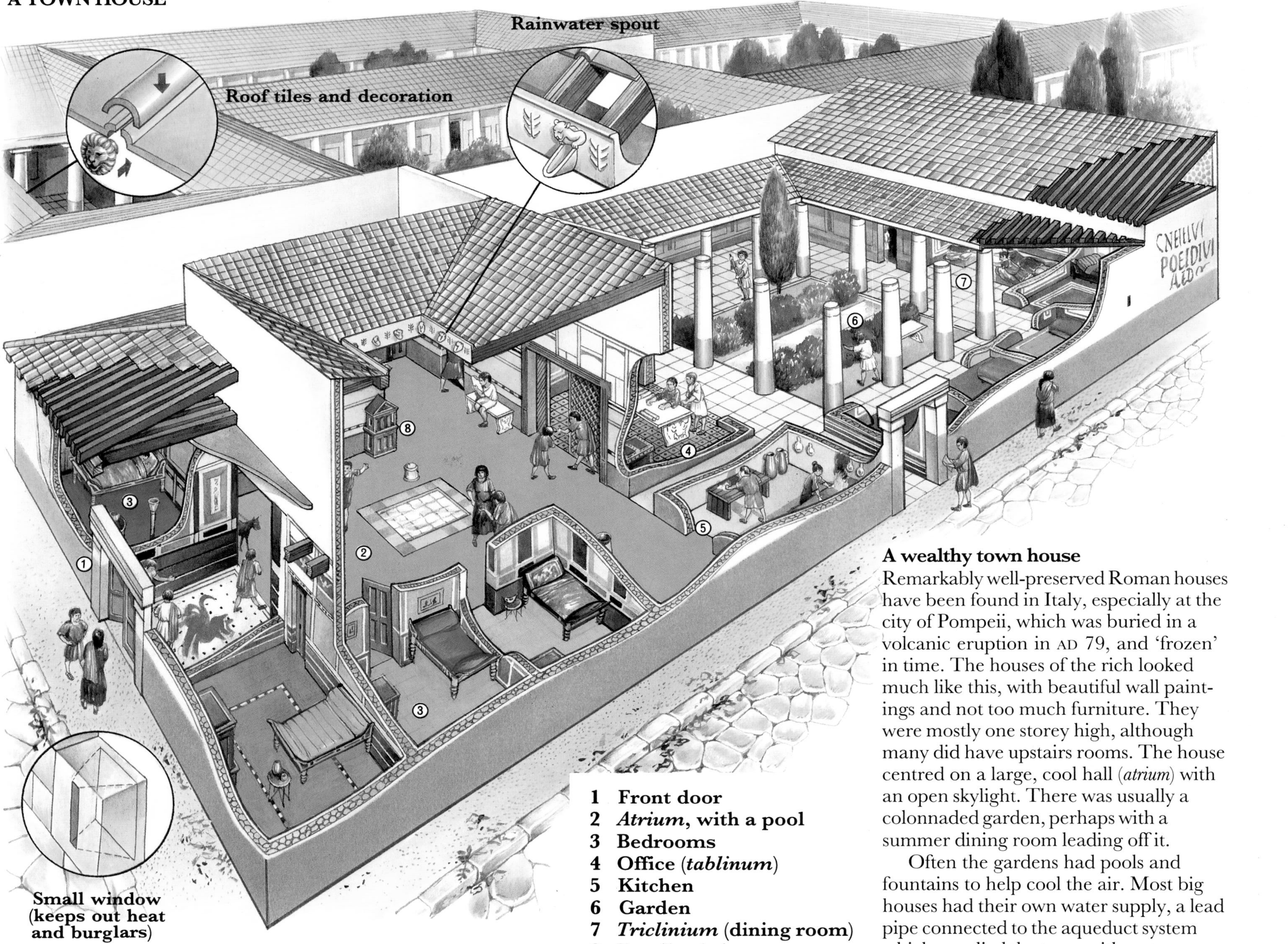

Rainwater spout

Roof tiles and decoration

Small window (keeps out heat and burglars)

A wealthy town house

Remarkably well-preserved Roman houses have been found in Italy, especially at the city of Pompeii, which was buried in a volcanic eruption in AD 79, and 'frozen' in time. The houses of the rich looked much like this, with beautiful wall paintings and not too much furniture. They were mostly one storey high, although many did have upstairs rooms. The house centred on a large, cool hall (*atrium*) with an open skylight. There was usually a colonnaded garden, perhaps with a summer dining room leading off it.

Often the gardens had pools and fountains to help cool the air. Most big houses had their own water supply, a lead pipe connected to the aqueduct system which supplied the town with water.

1 **Front door**
2 *Atrium*, **with a pool**
3 **Bedrooms**
4 **Office (***tablinum***)**
5 **Kitchen**
6 **Garden**
7 *Triclinium* **(dining room)**
8 **Family shrine**

Letters and documents were written in ink on papyrus rolls and sheets of wood, or scratched with a pointed stylus on reuseable wax-covered tablets.

This stone relief shows a shop which sells cushions and fabrics. The customer, evidently a rich lady, has been given a chair while she chooses what she likes.

Whatever work or business they did, Romans got up early, usually at dawn. They got dressed, had a light breakfast, and went about the day's work. In the houses of the wealthy, there would be much activity, especially if visitors were expected.

A MORNING'S BUSINESS

In wealthy households, it was a tradition that the family and slaves would come and wish the *paterfamilias* good morning. He would then begin the day by calling on his patron, or, if an important man himself, would receive his clients. After that, he might spend the morning looking at his accounts or writing letters, and discussing business affairs with his secretary.

OUT AND ABOUT

If a Roman's estates were close to the city, he might ride out to see the crops and inspect the livestock. He would probably go to the forum to hear the news and chat with friends, and perhaps make business deals, such as selling the produce of his lands, or chartering ships to send it overseas. If the man was a city councillor there might be meetings to attend, or, if he was a priest, there would be a temple to look after, and sacrifices to the gods to arrange and carry out. The magistrates for the year might be busy hearing law cases. Some Romans specialized as lawyers, and argued the case of a client before the magistrate, whether it concerned the technicalities of a disputed will, or the drama of a trial for murder.

SCHOOL AND SHOPPING

Meanwhile, the children from wealthy families would have gone to school, escorted by their pedagogue, or tutor. The mistress of the household would have given the servants their instructions for the day, and would perhaps be teaching her older daughters about skills such as housekeeping, spinning and weaving, in preparation for marriage. She might go to the market to buy household necessities or to see which luxuries had arrived from far-off places.

LUNCH

Everyone stopped for a lunch-break about noon. Also, during the longer days of summer, when the early afternoon was unbearably hot, most would have a short rest, a siesta. People in Mediterranean countries still do this today.

LEISURE

The better-off stopped work completely at lunchtime, although by then they had already had quite a long day. For them the afternoon was for relaxing at the baths, where again they would meet their friends and might invite people home for dinner. The evening meal was often quite a long affair, although usually it was followed by a fairly early bedtime.

For poor people and slaves the working day lasted until dusk, when they could stop work, eat dinner and go to bed. It was only the rich who could afford oil for lamps.

FEAST-DAYS AND HOLIDAYS

Romans did not have regular weekends. Instead there were many feast days which were holy to particular gods, or marked stages in the yearly cycle of summer and winter. Anniversaries of Emperors and famous men were also celebrated, with religious ceremonies and sometimes 'games'. Those who could took the day off to enjoy them. They were free, provided you could get a ticket, and this depended on knowing the right people.

Festivals, and the celebrations that went with them, provided a welcome change from the endless work of the yearly cycle. Even the slaves had a festival - the *Saturnalia*, which fell in December, when, just for a day, masters were supposed to serve the servants.

A scene on the main street of an Italian town. The shops and bars have opened their heavy wooden shutters for business. People are out shopping, dropping into the bar for a drink and a snack, or stopping at the public fountain to draw water. On the walls, people have been painting posters, advertising auctions, gladiator fights, and local elections. Note the stepping stones across the dirty street.

ROMANS AT WORK

People in Roman times worked very hard. The wealthy might work in government, the army or organizing their estates. Others had to do the menial work. Poorer families had to work all day to make enough to live on, and could rarely afford the luxury of a day off from work, perhaps to go to the games.

TRADES AND CRAFTS

Sons would often follow their fathers in whatever profession they had, whether it was baker or boatman, wine-seller or carpenter, weaver or wagon-driver, blacksmith or leather-worker.

There were very few professions open to women, although, for example, we do know of a few women doctors. Many women will have worked in their husband's shops, or perhaps earned extra money working at home doing traditional tasks like weaving.

Mosaic-making needed great skill. There were several methods. Often the pattern was marked out on the cement floor and the coloured stones quickly laid in the wet mortar, a small area at a time. Here the mosaic has been made earlier by glueing the stones onto a cloth. The finished panel has then been laid in mortar, and the cloth soaked and peeled off. Later the surface will be ground smooth and polished.

This stone relief shows a butcher at work, chopping up a joint of meat on a wooden block with a heavy iron cleaver. Hanging from the hooks are cuts of meat which have been prepared already, as in modern butchers' shops. Behind him, a kind of balance called a steelyard hangs on a pillar. It was used for weighing the meat.

SHOPS AND WORKSHOPS

There were many small businesses: some individual craftsmen sold their own produce directly to the public, or to traders who would sell the goods in other provinces. Shops and workshops have been found at Pompeii; they usually consist of a workshop and perhaps a small yard at the back, with a metal-worker's forge or a potter's kiln.

> **'A copper pot is missing from this shop. 65 sesterces reward if anyone brings it back, 20 sesterces if he reveals the thief so we can get our property back.'**
>
> — *A sign from Pompeii*

The shop at the front, opening onto the street, would have had a wooden or stone counter inside. There was no shop-window, because people liked to have as much air as possible in the hot Mediterranean climate. At night the shop was closed securely by a heavy sliding shutter. Many shops had a small flat upstairs where the craftsman and his family would have lived.

POTTERS AND KILNS

Few Roman businesses mass-produced like our modern factories, but some of the great pottery-making centres, the most famous of which were in France, operated in a similar way. There, factories made hundreds of thousands of fine red Samian pots. The potters were very skilled and could control the big kilns precisely. Inevitably, some pots were broken: if you visit these places today you are actually walking on thousands of fragments of Roman pots. Samian pottery was very fashionable and today can still be discovered all over the area of the Empire.

A NEW TECHNOLOGY

An important new craft in Roman times was glass-blowing. Ways of making glass had been known for centuries, but the idea of blowing glass bubbles and shaping them into useful things like bottles was a new one. It allowed glass to become a cheap, everyday material for the first time, and most people could afford some glass vessels.

Twisted rods of blue and white glass were sliced and pressed together in a mould to make this bowl. The yellow flagon was made by the new technique of glass-blowing: the basic bubble of hot glass was shaped by rolling it on a stone, and then the handle was made with an extra blob of molten glass, stuck on and shaped with pincers.

Iron was the most important material for making tools. The best Roman blacksmiths knew how to make it into tough steel. They could not make furnaces hot enough to melt it, so they hammered the hot metal into shape. For delicate objects such as jewellery, easily-worked gold, silver or brass were used.

PAINTERS AND MOSAICISTS

There was always a market for luxury goods among the wealthy. The very best craftsmen could make a good living by producing works of art for important people. Brilliantly-coloured wall-painting and mosaic-work were essential to great houses. It is thought that craftsmen had pattern books for customers to choose from.

MASONS AND BUILDERS

Stone-working was another major industry. Italy was fortunate in having many kinds of excellent building stone, and marble for statues and fine buildings. But, behind the marble, the real skill of Roman builders was hidden, for they had also invented an important new material - concrete, cleverly used with bricks. Concrete permitted the construction of huge vaults and covered spaces such as had never been seen before.

TRADE AND TRANSPORT

This is the Roman light-house at Dover. It originally had a large fire-beacon on top to signal to ships sailing in the English Channel.

A great variety of wheeled vehicles plied the roads of the Empire, for freight and passengers. This mosaic shows a heavy ox-cart. Lighter wagons had spoked wheels.

The conquest of the Empire brought in its wake the building of a vast road network. Equally important, the suppression of pirates who had long plagued the sea-lanes meant there was now safe passage across the Mediterranean Sea, the centre of the Roman world. These factors, plus the abolition of borders between countries, helped bring about a great increase in trade, and the movement of people, ideas and beliefs across the Empire.

IMPORTS AND EXPORTS

The early Empire was a time of increasing prosperity, and growing demand for all sorts of luxuries, many of them obtainable only from distant lands far to the East. For example, spices, Indian cottons and silks from mysterious China could now be bought in Rome. On the other hand, glass, red Samian pottery and other goods were traded to peoples outside the Empire. In fact, Roman silver coins have been found in India. Some Romans complained at the huge amounts of money flowing out of the country to the East.

ROADS AND HIGHWAYS

The roads built by the Romans are one of their most famous achievements, and today can still be traced in many places - indeed some are still in use. Often they run straight as an arrow for many kilometres, carried over swamps on causeways, running directly over hills or, if the hills were too steep, swerving round or tunnelling through them.

These highways were not actually built with traders in mind. They were built for the army, to move soldiers swiftly in time of war and to enable imperial messengers and officials to travel as easily and quickly as possible. Even so, news could only travel as fast as a person could carry a message on a horse. Warning of, say, a war on the Rhine would take several days to reach Rome. News from Syria or Egypt might take many weeks to arrive.

VEHICLES AND ANIMALS

Even the best roads had their problems; bandits, and snow and heavy rain in winter, could make the ways impassable. At the best of times, moving things by road was slow and expensive. Wagons and carriages were quite well-built, but heavy loads could only be pulled by lumbering oxen. Horses were faster, but the Romans had not worked out how to make an efficient horse-collar, so these animals could only pull light carriages, or be ridden.

Thus, road transport was really only suitable for travelling short distances, and for transporting small, expensive luxuries.

IKAPIOC

SHIPS AND SEALANES

Most goods, especially heavy cargoes of food, wine, oil, or marble, were moved by water. It was much cheaper and easier to haul heavy barges along rivers, or to sail freighters across the sea. The Mediterranean was the greatest of all the highways of the Empire, the winds carrying the produce of Egypt, Africa and Spain to the capital.

Voyages were swift if the wind was favourable, but they were unpredictable and often dangerous. In winter they stopped almost completely. Shipwreck was always a hazard. Even in summer, ships needed the wind to be in a certain direction and could be trapped in harbour for weeks awaiting suitable winds. Once at sea, ships' captains kept close to coasts to see where they were; they did not have compasses or accurate charts. Not surprisingly, sailors feared the gods and were very superstitious!

A ship laden with cargo approaches a busy harbour. Most vessels were small, carrying less than 200 tonnes of freight. Note the big steering oars at the stern.

23

BATHS

Equipment for a trip to the baths. The flask contains olive oil for rubbing onto the body. The curved strigil *is for scraping off the mixture of oil, dirt and sweat from the skin.*

Outside the baths there was usually an exercise yard, or, in colder climates such as Britain's, a large covered hall for games and work-outs.

The large Roman towns had many bath-houses. The richest houses might have their own private ones, but going to the baths was a social activity; most people liked to go out to bathe. Roman baths were similar to the modern Turkish ones, still found in a number of Arab countries. By visiting one today it is possible to get a good idea of what it must have been like in Roman baths, nearly 2,000 years ago.

SOCIAL BATHING

Roman baths were very unlike modern bath-rooms, or even swimming pools. There was much more to them, not least an exercise yard, where people could play ball-games or do weight-training. The bath-houses had the same role that bars do in Italy today; they were meeting places, where friends could talk and laugh or play board-games under the shady colonnade.

BATH BUILDINGS

The baths themselves were elaborate buildings, developed over many generations. They consisted of several vaulted rooms - cold, warm and hot, dry or humid - with changing rooms and other facilities.

Men and women bathed separately. Bigger bath-houses had a set of baths for each sex, but in smaller, poorer towns which could only afford one bath-house, people had to take turns. One inscription records that women went to the baths in the morning, to leave the favourite afternoon time for the men.

'I live over a bathing establishment. When the stronger fellows are exercising... I hear their groans... Add to this the arrest of a brawler or a thief, and the fellow who always likes to hear his own voice in the bath, and those who jump into the pool with a mighty splash.'

Seneca

Bath-houses varied enormously in size and reputation. Some were small, dark, seedy places, frequented by dubious characters. Even at the larger and more respectable baths, there was always the risk of thieves stealing clothes and money. Seneca's words paint a wonderful picture of the echoing noise, much like a modern swimming pool, to which were added the cries of vendors selling snacks and drinks.

IMPERIAL BATH-HOUSES

The greatest of all the baths were those built by the Emperors in the city of Rome. Those built by the Emperor Caracalla in the early third century covered 2 hectares! The baths of Diocletian, built a century later, were the greatest of all, and could hold about 2,000 people at a time. These establishments consumed huge quantities of fuel to keep them hot, and were so massive that it took weeks to heat them up.

A ROMAN BATH-HOUSE

1 Swimming pool
2 Exercise yard
3 Changing room (*apodyterium*)
4 Cold room (*frigidarium*)
5 Warm room (*tepidarium*)
6 Hot room (*caldarium*)
7 Heated pool
8 Hypocaust
9 Hot and cold water tanks

Taking a bath

This drawing is based on the Stabian baths at Pompeii. Here are the men's baths with the roof removed. The women's baths were to the right. Baths were complicated buildings, with a hypocaust, a floor raised on pillars. This allowed the hot gases from the heating fires to pass under the floors, and then through ducts in the walls and the concrete ceiling vaults. This meant that the heated rooms received warmth from the walls and ceiling as well as through the floors. Bathers had to wear wooden sandals to avoid getting burnt feet! The water in the warm pools was heated in a similar way.

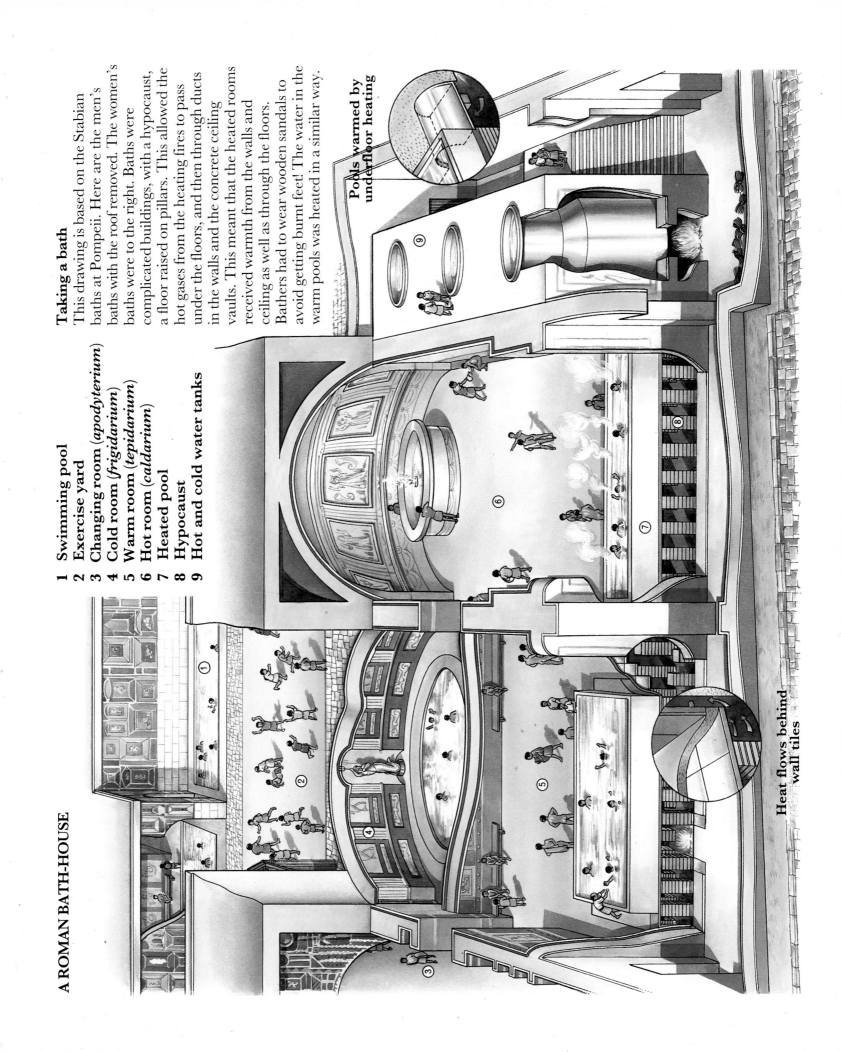

Pools warmed by underfloor heating

Heat flows behind wall tiles

FOOD AND DINING

Glass bottles like these were used in kitchens, probably for storing ingredients such as honey, or expensive sauces.

A portable water-heater, beautifully made in bronze. Water from the big tank on the left flowed into the horse-shoe-shaped jacket around a brazier, in which charcoal was burned to provide the heat.

The Romans are notorious for orgies of over-eating, and for serving amazing dishes, but this view is much exaggerated. Indeed there are descriptions of great banquets which live up to this reputation, but they were untypical even of rich Romans. Most ordinary people had a fairly ordinary diet, and could only dream of sampling delicate foods.

FOODS AND DIET

Nutrition was not very well understood, and it was often difficult for most ordinary town-dwellers to get very fresh food. In the winter-time in the northern provinces, fresh vegetables, meat and fruit were almost unobtainable, leading to poor health. Some foods were preserved by smoking, drying, salting or pickling. Nevertheless, a lot of the food available was probably almost rotten by the time it was eaten, so it is not really surprising that herbs and strong-tasting sauces like *garum* (fish sauce) were popular; they were used to disguise the poor taste.

Many of the foods we take for granted today were not known in the Roman world, but came to the Mediterranean centuries later. For example Romans had never heard of potatoes, oranges, lemons, bananas, tea or coffee.

The poor had to live on 'take-aways', because few had kitchens. They bought bread from stalls and big bakeries, provisions from the market, and hot food from the many bars in town. In Rome itself, the Emperors helped the poor by providing some free food to families, and the city came to depend on the arrival of the annual grain fleet bringing the wheat of Egypt. If it was delayed, there could be riots by discontented citizens waiting for the ships.

One of the many street bars and food shops still to be seen in the ruined streets of Roman towns such as Pompeii, or in this case Herculaneum. Large jars are set into the serving counter, perhaps as wine coolers or for live shellfish.

MEALTIMES

Romans had several mealtimes during the day. Breakfast was usually very light, perhaps consisting of no more than bread and water. Lunch at around noon was more substantial, and might include meat, fish and fruit, with wine. For most, the main meal of the day was dinner (*cena*), late in the afternoon, at the end of the working day after a visit to the baths. Wealthy people would often invite friends or clients to come to dinner.

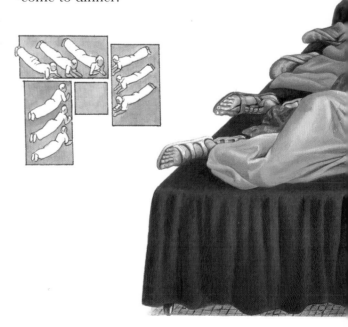

GOOD FOOD, GOOD COMPANY

Dinner parties in big houses could be drunken, rowdy affairs with dancers and clowns, but they were often cultured, frugal events, with the host providing fine wines and simple but tasty dishes. There would be conversation on philosophy, politics or literature. Sometimes an educated slave would read poetry to entertain the guests.

We know of one Roman who thought he was a great poet. He would invite all his friends to his house for dinner, and make them listen to his terrible poems while they ate their food. As his guests, they had to try to be polite.

Dinners usually consisted of numerous small dishes, in three courses. There were simple starters such as eggs, lettuce, olives, snails, oysters or even sea urchins. The main courses included fish or meat dishes, often with rich sauces. Known recipes include 'Trojan Pig', a pig stuffed with several other meats and sausages. The tables of the great might boast exotic dishes such as peacock and ostrich.

Food was usually eaten from shared dishes, with a spoon or more often with the fingers. Small knives might also be used.

Wine was drunk from small cups of fine pottery, or silver. Metal cups could make the wine taste unpleasant, so glass cups became increasingly popular. All sorts of wines were served, from heavy red vintages to thin whites. They were usually watered down for serving, and might be chilled with ice (difficult to get in a world without refrigerators), or flavoured with honey and other substances. Spirits were not yet invented, but beer was a popular drink north of the Alps. It seems that only children and invalids drank milk.

The kitchen of a big house. Food was cooked on a sort of hob (centre). Metal vessels were stood on iron stands over charcoal, rather like a barbecue. Note the tall wine jar, and the glass and pottery storage vessels.

In the dining room, the triclinium, *three couches were arranged around the table, with one side open for servants to bring dishes in and out. Nine was thought to be the ideal number of diners, with three per couch, although sometimes even more were squeezed in.*

RELIGION AND GODS

A marble relief of the Eastern god Mithras, from a temple of the cult. It shows the god slaying the holy bull, whose blood was believed to have brought life to the world.

Most Romans believed deeply in the power of the gods, and that it was important to pay attention to omens. This relief shows a procession of animals being led to sacrifice, to bring about harmony with the gods. Note the axe which would be used during the ceremony.

The peoples of the Roman world worshipped a variety of different gods, and they were allowed to do so as long as they also paid homage to the official gods of the Roman state. The most important of these were Jupiter, who was king of the gods; Juno, his wife; Minerva, the goddess of wisdom; Roma, the goddess of Rome; and the guardian spirit (the *genius*) of the Emperor.

THE EMPEROR AS GOD
It was thought natural by some of the peoples of the Roman Empire to worship the Emperor as a living god, as they had always worshipped their rulers, but this was frowned upon by many Romans. Most Emperors were declared to have become gods when they died, however. When he was on his deathbed, the Emperor Vespasian joked 'Oh dear, I seem to be becoming a god!'

GODS GREAT AND SMALL
The Romans usually honoured the gods of the peoples they conquered. The old gods of the Greeks were still important in the East, although they became virtually indistinguishable from the Roman gods: Jupiter was the same as the Greek god Zeus; the god of war, Mars, corresponded to the Greek god Ares; the goddess of love, Venus, and the Greek goddess Aphrodite were the same; and so on.

There were also hundreds of local deities, guardian goddesses of cities, gods of sacred places, etc. Particular gods watched over certain trades and activities, Mercury watching over travel, for example. And individual homes and families had their own private gods and protective spirits, including those of the family ancestors.

FESTIVALS
Then, as now, people worshipped their gods on holy days (hence 'holidays') and festivals, of which there were many. There was no seven-day week with a holy day of rest, except among the Jews, at this time.

HOLY MYSTERIES
People prayed and made sacrifice in times of trouble or illness, but many found the old religions dull and unrewarding, and lacking in spiritual fulfilment. Traditional

28

cults offered little hope for an afterlife other than as a spirit in a gloomy underworld. Some of the more exotic religions of the East, however, offered hope of eternal life and seemed to give more meaning to often sad or hopeless lives in this world.

A number of these cults spread across the Empire, moving along trade routes with travellers. Among the most popular were those of the Egyptian goddess Isis and the Persian god Mithras. These religions involved secret initiation ceremonies, revelations of sacred 'mysteries' (holy secrets), and the promise of rebirth in an afterlife.

JEWS AND CHRISTIANS

The Romans have a largely undeserved reputation for religious intolerance, mainly because of the horrific persecution of Christians and terrible wars with the Jews. These clashes were caused by the fact that the two religions, Judaism and Christianity, were fundamentally different from the many other tolerated religions.

The Jews were mostly a separate national community, still largely based in Palestine. Normally it was agreed that the Jews would pray to their god for the Emperor. However, some Romans did not understand that Judaism forbade sacrifice to the official Roman deities, and they caused rebellion by demanding obedience.

The beliefs of the Christians, too, forbade worship of the Roman gods. To the Emperors this seemed to endanger the Empire, by risking the anger of the official Roman gods. Also, the early Christians worshipped in relative secrecy, which meant that other people believed they were hiding something. They were even falsely accused of eating humans, or cannibalism. Therefore, in times of trouble, the small numbers of Christians were an easy target for the anger of ignorant people, who wanted someone to blame, and many were tortured or killed. But the Christians' faith was only strengthened by persecution, and their courage was admired by many.

The end of a Roman wedding day. After the religious ceremony, which usually took place at the bride's house, she was traditionally taken in torchlit procession to her husband's house. This would become her home. On arrival he would greet her, and she would be carried over the threshold, a tradition which has lasted down to modern times.

29

CHARIOTS AND GLADIATORS

A bronze gladiator's helmet, elaborately decorated with animals and faces. It was meant to look splendid, and it offered good protection. However, it limited vision, making it harder for the gladiator to fight a swift opponent.

Roman cities had places of entertainment where, during festivals and on other special occasions, games were staged. These included plays and shows in the theatre, and chariot racing. As befitted the capital, the most spectacular events were held in Rome itself.

ENTERTAINMENT

The larger cities had special race-tracks, called circuses, for chariot racing. The infamous wild beast hunts, and fights between gladiators, took place in a special oval arena called an amphitheatre. Many thousands of people and animals were killed to entertain the spectators.

Originally all these performances, amusing, exciting or horrible, were put on for religious reasons - there were plays and races to honour the gods, and gladiator fights at the funerals of great men. By the early Empire they were held simply to amuse the people, often being sponsored by rich Romans to get popularity and be elected to important jobs. Much of the entertainment in Rome was organized at the Emperor's command.

A Roman charioteer of the 'red' stable with a race-horse. He carries a whip, and wears a helmet and protective leather armour in case of a crash.

THUNDERING HOOVES

Chariot racing was probably the most popular of the games. One reason was that families could sit together; at gladiator fights and plays, women had to sit at the back. Apparently men thought they might run off with a handsome actor or fighter!

A marble relief showing a chariot thundering down the circus straight. The obelisks and lap-counters which decorated the central barrier of the track are behind. The figures on the right are race officials, with the magnificent arched starting gates beyond them.

CHARIOTS AND CHARIOTEERS

The chariots were lightly built for maximum speed, and were usually pulled by four horses, although two, three and other numbers of horse could be harnessed. The charioteers were often very young and had to be strong. The reins were tied around their waists so that they would not drop them, although in the event of a crash they would be dragged along the ground, and many were killed.

ON THE TRACK

Four or eight chariots of the different teams competed in each race. At Rome there were four teams: the Blues, Greens, Whites and Reds each had fans much like modern football teams. Successful charioteers were popular heroes; people knew all the best horses, and made bets on the outcomes of the many races.

The race began when the gates opened to release the teams from the starting traps. Seven laps were run, anti-clockwise around the track. There were very few rules, and collisions and injuries were common. After thundering across the finishing line, the winner was awarded a crown and palm leaf of victory, and often a large cash prize.

BLOOD IN THE SAND

The amphitheatre was a much grimmer place, where the 'games' lasted several days. Most gladiators were slaves or convicts condemned to fight. In the mornings, there were usually fights between animals, or between 'hunters' and fierce lions or other big cats. At lunchtime, some clowns might provide the entertainment, or there might be some public executions.

The highlight of the day was in the afternoon, when the gladiators fought to the death, usually in single combats between different types. The nimble *retiarius*, for instance, armed with only a trident and weighted net, often fought with the massively armoured but lumbering *myrmillo*.

DEATH AND GLORY

When a gladiator was wounded he could appeal for mercy. If he had fought well it might be granted, but the crowd could turn their thumbs down, and shout *'iugula!'* ('cut his throat!'), and the victor would dispatch him. Some men became experts at this gruesome work; one gladiator had 88 victories. Some gladiators became popular heroes and won their freedom from the arena - some missed the excitement, however, and agreed to fight again.

People enjoyed the bloodshed, but were easily bored by repetition. They relished novelties, such as women gladiators, war-chariots from far-off Britain, and even 'naval battles' in flooded arenas.

A heavy gladiator fights a retiarius. The retiarius has dropped his weighted net and so cannot trip his lumbering opponent, and now must rely on his speed and agility to survive.

THE THEATRE

Actors' masks, which had large mouths to speak through, can often be seen in mosaics and sculptures.

Theatre was a Greek invention. Greek plays were originally religious rites, holy to the god Dionysus. The main types of theatre were tragedy and comedy, and the actors, who were always men, wore character-masks. Performances in the open air took place in special buildings, with seating for thousands.

PANTOMIME

The Romans adopted theatre with great enthusiasm and were soon writing and performing plays of their own. The plays were often based on original Greek plays, with Greek characters, and performed by Greek actors. The plays eventually lost most of their religious connections.

The Romans invented a type of performance called pantomime, similar to ballet or to the complex and beautiful dancing of India. The actors portrayed famous tales of gods and mortals by the clever use of movement and gesture, and with many changes of mask and costume.

PLOTS AND CHARACTERS

Other types of Roman performances were more light-hearted. The most famous Roman playwrights were Plautus and Terence. They wrote comedies about characters people could laugh at, or feel pity for, such as old misers, swaggering soldiers, wronged daughters and, almost always, the scheming slave who gets his come-uppance at the end. Masks were used in these plays. As in Greece, all characters, including females, were played by men.

'It sharpens the wits, it exercises the body, it delights the spectator, it instructs him in the history of bygone days... while eye and ear are held beneath the spell of flute and cymbal and of graceful dance... I say nothing of the excellent moral influence of public opinion... you will find the evil-doer greeted with curses and his victim with sympathetic tears.'

——— Lucian on pantomime and theatre ———

THE ACTOR'S LOT

Actors had a difficult task because audiences were often many thousands strong, and did not always sit and listen politely. Greek and Roman theatres were built to carry the actors' voices to the highest seats, but people still tended to get bored easily. And rumours of something interesting happening elsewhere could cause a noisy exit of some of the audience.

People had mixed feelings about actors. Many were very popular, but Roman nobles felt that they were a bad influence on people's morals - for example, during the Republic, the senate had prevented the building of permanent theatres altogether.

A mosaic from Pompeii showing actors in their dressing-room, putting on costumes and rehearsing for a performance. The figure in the middle is practising a tune on the pipes.

32

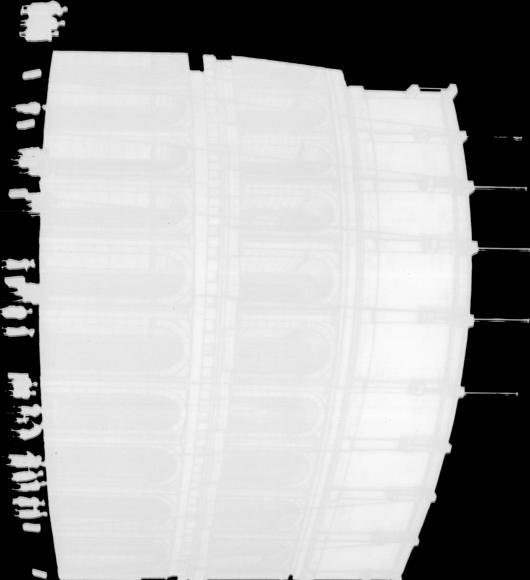

A ROMAN THEATRE

At the theatre

This splendid Roman theatre is of the type seen in Italy and many of the Mediterranean provinces. It could hold several thousand people. Its deep, semicircular shape and the sloping roof above the stage meant that even those high up at the back could hear the actors clearly - provided the crowd kept quiet! The stage often had an elaborate backdrop (the *scenae frons*) decorated with marble columns, statues and mosaics. It represented three house-fronts, and the actors entered and exited through the doors. Actors could perform on stage and in an area in front called the *orchestra*. The seating for the audience was supported on elaborately-constructed concrete vaults and arches.

Archway construction

1 Stage and actors
2 Stage backdrop (*scenae frons*)
3 Actors performing in the *orchestra*
4 Sloping roof
5 Dressing rooms and stores
6 Ramp
7 Stairs
8 Concrete vaults
9 Gallery
10 Movable sunshade (*velarium*)
11 Guy ropes

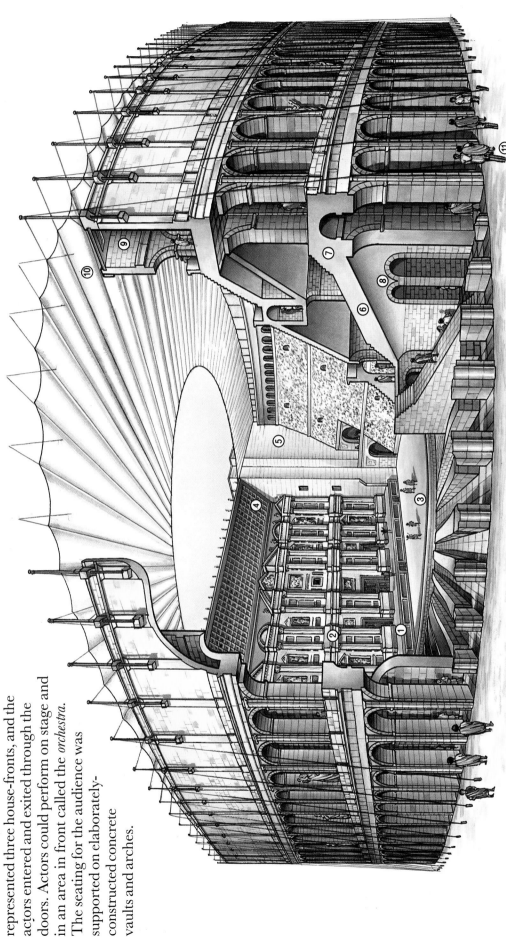

DEATH AND BURIAL

Roman law decreed that people were buried outside city walls, and so large cemeteries surrounded the cities, and graves lined the roadsides. Graves were often marked by monuments, with Latin inscriptions. Since the family and their ancestors were very important to the Romans, their tombs reflected this: monuments on the graves of the wealthy were extravagantly decorated with marble. The poor probably just had wooden grave markers.

DEAD MEN'S TALES

Tombstones can tell us a great deal about individual Romans. Careful study of the skeletons found can tell us, for example, how tall they were, roughly how old they were when they died, and their general state of health during life. Physical injuries and periods of malnutrition can also be detected. This information helps to build up a picture of Roman life and death. Unfortunately, many graves had long since been looted and destroyed.

DISEASE AND CURE

Ancient writings, too, tell us a lot about how and why people died. Medicine was limited, and only available to the rich. The Romans were not very clean people and did not know about bacteria or understand how illnesses were passed on. Many believed that illnesses were caused by the anger of the gods or even witchcraft, and a religious or magical cure was often sought. People would pray and sacrifice to a god, such as the Greek healing god Asklepios, or visit shrines to seek a cure.

HAZARDS OF LIFE

Illnesses and injuries, routinely treated today, were certain death in Roman times. No vaccinations, terrible poverty and poor diet meant that many children died soon after birth. Those who survived to adulthood faced the risks of epidemics and accidents. Diseases of the stomach and the eyes were common, largely due to poor hygiene. Childbirth was dangerous and many women died giving birth. Roman women probably stood less than a 50 per cent chance of reaching 40 years old, and men's life expectancy was not much greater - although some Romans lived to their eighties and beyond.

This tombstone of a young boy from a wealthy family was found at Ostia, near Rome. He is shown holding a goat, which might be a family pet or an animal intended for sacrifice to the gods.

Some rich people, especially those who owned family burial vaults, were buried in great marble coffins called sarcophagi. These were usually magnificently carved with religious or mythical scenes. This example depicts a battle between Romans and barbarians: in the tangle of horses, soldiers and bodies, the artist has captured the chaos of war.

PYRES AND SEPULCHRES

When someone died the body was usually burnt on a pyre (cremated), and the ashes placed in a jar in the family tomb, or buried in the ground. Food and perhaps the person's favourite items, such as jewellery, would be buried with the ashes. Later it became fashionable just to bury the body, without cremation. The rich were sometimes buried in family vaults in magnificent carved stone coffins, called sarcophagi.

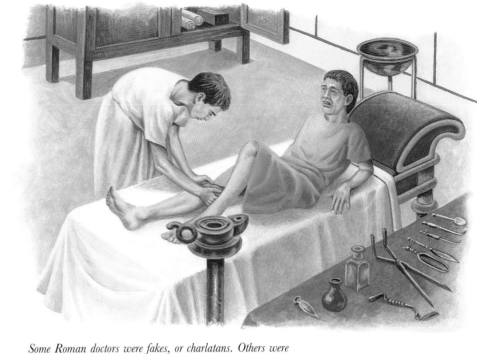

Some Roman doctors were fakes, or charlatans. Others were very skilled in the use of their special medical instruments and the medicines available. But they knew there were many things they could not do. They had no real anaesthetics, so operations were terrifying, agonizing and perilous.

Roman funerals could be very grand affairs, with professional mourners hired to wail over the body. The funeral processions of Roman nobles included people wearing masks depicting the dead person's famous ancestors.

PEOPLES OF THE PROVINCES

A jewelled gold disc and necklace from Roman Egypt, very similar to jewellery worn all over the Empire. In Roman times, fashions and ideas spread widely, and were shared all over the Empire.

The Roman Empire was an astonishing mosaic of peoples, of which only a tiny minority were Italian. In addition to the Latin-speaking Italians and Greek-speaking cities of the East, there were the Celtic Gauls of France, Dacians on the River Danube, and the Syrians, Egyptians, and many others.

COMMON TONGUES

The Empire incorporated almost all of the Greek-speaking world, centred on the Aegean Sea, but scattered in many long-established cities from the Eastern desert to the southern shores of France. While Latin and Greek became the standard languages for communication, business, law and government, hundreds of other tongues were spoken, from Egyptian dialects and Aramaic in the East, to Celtic and early German in the North West.

LANDS AND NATIONS

Their varied landscapes, climates, histories and cultures, meant that the Empire's provinces looked very different from each other, although all were criss-crossed by roads and dotted with cities. And pictures and descriptions of their people show a variety of appearances, from black Africans on the southern fringes of Egypt to dark Syrians and red-headed or blond Gauls and Britons.

For people who lived in the provinces, daily life was not changed much by the Roman conquest, except that wars were less frequent and new taxes had to be paid. They normally kept their own laws and spoke their own languages. In some areas, especially remote mountain lands, even centuries of Roman rule left little mark.

ROMANIZING THE EMPIRE

In other areas, slowly but surely, profound changes took place, as Greco-Roman ways spread to more and more people. Latin gradually replaced many other languages in the West, and in medieval times developed into modern languages such as French and Spanish, as well as Italian.

As they became more and more like the Romans, many people began to think of themselves as Romans. Indeed, the Emperors were generous in making people from the provinces into Roman citizens. Eventually, almost everyone in the Empire was legally a Roman citizen, whether they were Syrian soldiers, Greek priestesses, or British farmers. For the only period in the history of the Mediterranean world, it was united into a single state, and was at peace.

Farmers paying their taxes in Gaul. The early Empire did not have thousands of government tax-collectors, but got the city councils to collect revenues. This worked quite well, but was often not so good for ordinary people. The city councillors who collected the taxes were mostly rich local landowners. Thus a farmer's taxman was also often his landlord! It seems many councillors demanded extra money which they kept for themselves, and there was little the taxpayer could do about it.

TRADERS AND MIGRANTS

The Roman Peace made the seas and the roads much safer for traders and travellers. Many people migrated in search of their fortunes, or fled troubles at home, or were shipped to other countries as slaves. Many Jews, for example, left their homeland and settled in other provinces; and Syrians migrated to the great trading centre of Lugdunum in Gaul (now the French city of Lyon). Of course Rome attracted the most immigrants, and almost every language spoken in the Empire could be heard there.

FLOWERING OF THE PROVINCES

As time passed, the wealthy populations of each province became increasingly like each other. Provincials became not just citizens, but equestrians and even senators. By the third century AD, men of provincial origin were reaching the throne itself. Thus the provinces were quietly 'conquering' Italy, as the affairs of the Roman world passed more and more into the hands of non-Italians, and the major political events took place in the East or the North.

Rich Romans hunted all over the provinces, and in the lands beyond, for exotic animals. These were taken to Rome to fight in the arena. Here a hunted tigress is pictured in a mosaic from Sicily.

A market scene in a trading city on the fringes of the Syrian desert. In cities such as Palmyra, East met West in an exotic blend of Greek, Roman and oriental language, customs and architecture. Through such places, spices and silks arrived from the Far East.

EMPERORS AND GOVERNORS

The city-states which made up the Empire were governed by their own councils, which collected the taxes and kept law and order for the Roman government. The cities of a region were then grouped together into provinces, large and small, under Roman governors. These governors were responsible to the supreme ruler, the Emperor, and the senate at Rome.

THE REINS OF POWER
In theory, the Roman senate was in charge of government, and so the governors of the provinces were selected from the senators. In practice, however, all real power was in the hands of the Emperor. He 'looked after' the frontier provinces for the senate - which meant that he controlled all the big armies, which were the ultimate source of power, and appointed deputies to be governors on his behalf. These men, who served for about three years, were mostly senators. They were very powerful (the governor of Britain commanded an army of up to 50,000 men), and there was always the danger of a rebellion. Therefore the Emperors had to watch them carefully.

GOVERNORS AND PROCURATORS
To be a governor it was necessary to have been a magistrate in the city of Rome and an officer in the army legions. Governors had to keep order, command the troops if there was a war, and act as chief judge for their allotted province. Crimes which were punishable by death, or involved Roman citizens, were tried by the governor, who visited the major cities of his province to hold court there.

The other important official in the province was the procurator, who dealt with taxes. Like the governor, the procurator was a wealthy citizen - a businessman rather than a senator. His job was to organize the collection of taxes, pay the soldiers, and send money to the Emperor.

CORRUPTION AND RETRIBUTION
Many Roman officials were corrupt, and took bribes or simply stole from the people they governed. Sometimes this led to serious trouble, most famously the rebellion of the Britons under Queen Boudica (Boadicea). Emperors tried to keep the officials under control, and many were prosecuted when they returned to Rome.

A large brass coin (called a sestertius) of the Emperor Nero, who reigned from AD 54 to 68. Around his portrait the writing gives his name, titles and honours: 'Nero Claudius Caesar Augustus, victor over the Germans, Chief Priest... three times victorious general.'

Although early Emperors were senators, and people pretended that the senate was the main government, real power depended on the army's support. Emperors are often shown addressing the soldiers, as in this second century relief, to which the fourth century Emperor Constantine has added his own head!

RULERS OF THE ROMAN WORLD

Augustus, the first Emperor, was a senator, as were his successors. Some of them ruled wisely and well, and tried to look after the people of the provinces. Others are infamous for their cruelty. Many of the worst had grown up as princes in the royal palace, knowing they could do as they pleased; it seems this sent some of them mad. Nero, who ruled from AD 54 until AD 68, is probably the best known. He believed he was a great athlete and artist, and it was rumoured that he deliberately started the Great Fire of AD 64 which burned much of Rome to the ground.

Hadrian's Wall, the greatest fortification ever built by the Roman army, ran for 120 kilometres from sea to sea across northern England. Here a Governor (centre) and his escort of legionaries is preparing to inspect the wall.

CONQUERORS AND GUARDIANS

Other Emperors started terrible wars of conquest. Trajan, for example, conquered Dacia (approximately modern Rumania) and invaded the Parthian empire to the East. However, his friend and more famous successor Hadrian spent his reign touring the Empire, to inspect the armies and provinces. During his visit to Britain in AD 122, he ordered the building of the great wall which is named after him today. It was probably constructed to improve the defences of the province, and perhaps to keep the unruly soldiers busy!

Hadrian, and his successors Antoninus Pius and Marcus Aurelius, were some of the better Emperors, who did their best to keep the peace and to protect the Empire. Under later Emperors, civil war broke out in the provinces, and the Empire suffered.

A marble bust of the Emperor Trajan, one of the last of the great conquering Emperors.

39

A SOLDIER'S LIFE

Roman soldiers did not spend all of their time on campaigns. In winter months, and the summers if there was no war, they stayed mostly in army bases. We know quite a lot about Roman forts, because many have been excavated by archaeologists.

THE PLAN OF A FORT

Army bases varied in size, from quite small forts holding a single regiment of auxiliaries (like the one shown here), to vast legionary bases covering 20 hectares. However, they all had similar layouts, and the same types of building. In Europe, the forts of the early Empire were usually rectangular, with rounded corners, like a playing card.

In the middle of the fort, facing the main gate, stood the headquarters building. This was where the regimental standards were kept. It had a large staff of clerks to carry out the everyday business of the regiment, such as the writing of reports and letters, and there were also engineers and surveyors. The headquarters was flanked by the commander's house, large granaries for the soldiers' food, and perhaps workshops or a hospital.

A Roman auxiliary cavalryman. The cavalry saddle, of Celtic origin, was not widespread until the early Empire. Cavalry horses do not seem to have had horseshoes.

Boots were very important to Roman soldiers, who had to march up to 30 kilometres a day. They wore heavy sandals with iron hob-nails for toughness. The open leatherwork kept the feet healthy.

A typical Roman 800-man auxiliary fort, with a civilian settlement outside the wall. York, the second city of England, started as a village outside the walls of a fort. The see-through picture shows part of the fort in detail.

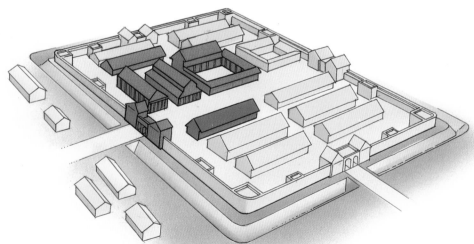

SOLDIERS' QUARTERS

Most of the fort was filled with barrack blocks, where the soldiers lived in cramped conditions, eight men to a room, one 'century' of soldiers (actually 80 men) to a block. Each block had a small 'bungalow' at the end for the centurion. Soldiers might spend as long as 20 years in the same room with the same comrades, so they had to get on well! Some cavalry forts had stable blocks, but most horses lived outside the walls. Surrounding the fort there were many other buildings, including a bath-house and usually a village.

THE ROMAN SOLDIER

Soldiers were paid quite well, but could not go away on leave to spend it, so traders set up shop outside the gates of the fort. There would also have been taverns, where the men could drink and gamble. There was probably frequent trouble, but the soldiers had to be careful; military punishments were very harsh. The soldiers often married local women; the families lived close to the fort or in the village.

AN AUXILIARY FORT

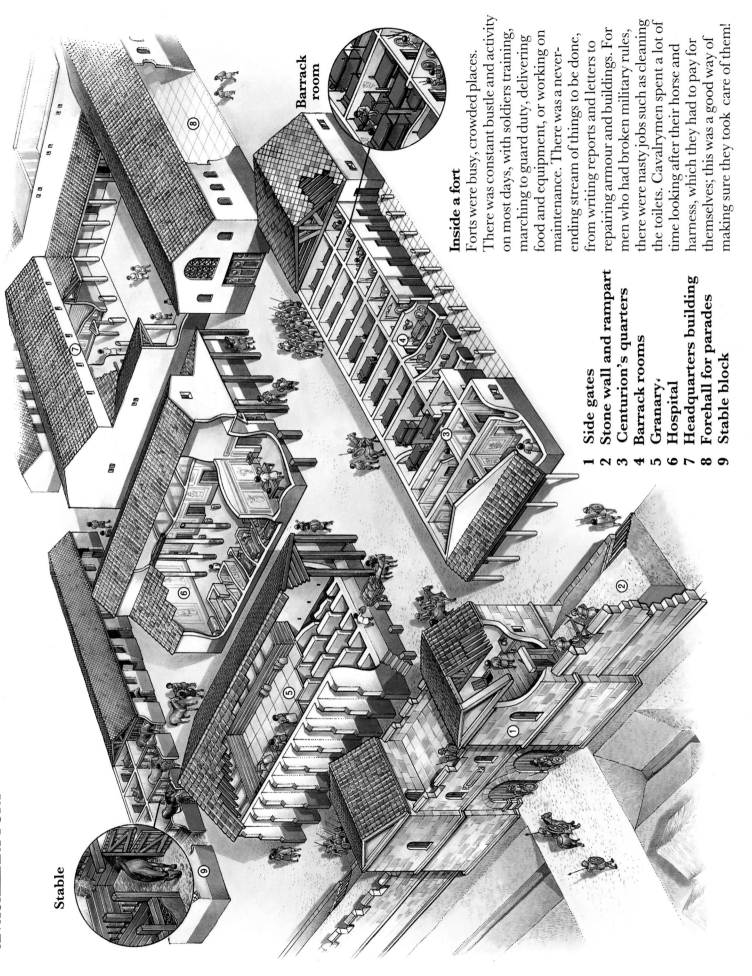

Stable

Barrack room

Inside a fort

Forts were busy, crowded places. There was constant bustle and activity on most days, with soldiers training, marching to guard duty, delivering food and equipment, or working on maintenance. There was a never-ending stream of things to be done, from writing reports and letters to repairing armour and buildings. For men who had broken military rules, there were nasty jobs such as cleaning the toilets. Cavalrymen spent a lot of time looking after their horse and harness, which they had to pay for themselves; this was a good way of making sure they took care of them!

1 **Side gates**
2 **Stone wall and rampart**
3 **Centurion's quarters**
4 **Barrack rooms**
5 **Granary**
6 **Hospital**
7 **Headquarters building**
8 **Forehall for parades**
9 **Stable block**

In the first and second centuries AD, most people in the Empire saw little of the army and were untroubled by war for most of their lives. The army was successful in defending the frontiers against the foreign tribes to the North, and the Parthian Empire to the East.

The Roman legion had a large number of catapults, which were used mainly for sieges. They were powered by twisted 'springs' of rope or sinew, and could hurl projectiles several hundred metres. Most were light arrow-shooters, like giant crossbows. Bigger catapults hurled stones.

DEFENDING THE EMPIRE

The army kept a careful watch on the borders, using patrols and systems of forts, and sometimes barriers. Diplomats tried to keep foreigners friendly, or encouraged them to fight each other. If spies or patrols detected trouble brewing, the Romans planned to attack first.

NEW CONQUESTS

Sometimes new lands were conquered and became part of the Empire, such as southern Britain in AD 43, or Dacia at the start of the second century, but for the most part the Romans were content to hold all the lands west of the River Rhine, and south of the River Danube in Europe.

The Romans had, in fact, expanded about as far as they could. They discovered that it was difficult to conquer lands which had only a small population and little productive agricultural land, such as the forests of Germany, the grasslands of the Asian Steppe, or the Arabian deserts, where the legions were unable to maintain themselves. The Empire stopped expanding, and the second century AD was quite peaceful, despite the tribes of the North pressing increasingly on its frontiers.

'Possessing the best part of the earth and sea... They surround the Empire with great armies, and they garrison the whole stretch of land and sea like a single stronghold.'

— *Appian, Roman History* —

ON THE MARCH

The Roman army on campaign was a fearsome machine. Columns of troops, sometimes kilometres long, trudged into enemy lands, the legions clearing the way, building temporary bridges and camps. Legions contained experts and craftsmen who could make or build almost anything the army needed. They were accompanied by a great train of wagons with catapults and supplies. The auxiliaries scouted far and wide to locate the enemy and to search for ambushes. Parties were sent out to gather food and fuel, while others were despatched to burn villages, forcing the enemy out to face them on the battlefield.

THE HEAT OF BATTLE

In battle the lines of soldiers faced each other before charging in for hand-to-hand combat. The legions bore the brunt of the fighting. They were heavily armoured, and carried fearsome javelins which punched through the enemy's shields. Their short swords were used to stab, inflicting terrible wounds. Roman poets wrote of the glory of war, but the reality was very bloody and terrifying. Once the legions had forced the enemy to retreat, or run away, the cavalry would give chase and cut them down. If the enemy's leader was captured, he would be taken to Rome and killed.

SKILL AND STRATEGY

Many Roman generals were experts at their trade, and won wars by skill rather than simple brute force and bloodshed. They sometimes won cheaply and quickly, by moving troops very fast to surprise the enemy. Julius Caesar was famous for this tactic, and was also good at guessing what his opponents would do; faced with a vast Gallic army, he did not attack, as he knew the Gauls were not very good at supplying their troops with food - he simply waited until the Gauls got hungry and went home!

PART-TIME GENERALS

Most generals, however, were not professional soldiers, but senators who took the job as part of their career of public service. The army was designed to cope with this. The tough and experienced centurions commanded the troops in action, and even a bad general could win battles.

The Roman army was not invincible, of course, and there were disasters: in AD 9, three legions were massacred in Germany. But for centuries the Roman army was remarkably effective at conquest and at defending the Empire.

Here Roman legionaries are in a desperate fight with some 'barbarians' on the northern frontier of the Empire. The strict battle lines the Romans normally kept have become disordered, but the legionaries' big shields and iron armour are giving them good protection. A unit of fresh troops is coming to the rescue.

43

A CHANGING WORLD

In the years around AD **150**, Rome was at the zenith of her power and the Roman world was generally peaceful and prosperous. But this situation did not last. There was growing trouble on the Northern frontiers, and the army found it increasingly difficult to keep the 'barbarian' tribes out. These foreign peoples, mostly Germans, wanted to enter the Empire - to plunder, or to settle and to share in the fabulous civilization to the South.

These statues are of the Emperor Diocletian and the three deputy-emperors he appointed to bring peace back to the Roman world. The statues show these tough soldier-emperors as equal and united against their enemies. They are so similar that we do not know which one is meant to be Diocletian himself!

CIVIL WAR

In the mid-third century AD, a series of violent civil wars broke out, as generals fought for the throne. Thus the Roman Empire was already sinking into chaos when a new crisis arose in the East. An aggressive new Persian Empire overthrew the old Parthian state and attacked Rome. With the Germans attacking from the North, the Romans now found themselves fighting desperately on two fronts.

DISASTER AND RECOVERY

A long series of civil wars and disasters on the frontiers of the Empire took place in the mid-third century AD, which led to the break-up of the Empire into several pieces. Astonishingly, against all odds, a succession of ruthlessly efficient soldier-emperors reunited the Empire, suppressed the warring generals, and drove out the invaders.

The greatest of these Emperors was Diocletian, who became Emperor in AD 284. One of the last pagan Emperors, he brought order and stability back to Rome and, like Augustus 300 years before, overhauled everything from the army to the government and the coinage.

THE LATE EMPIRE

It was a very different Empire that emerged from the crises of the third century: the government was harsh, and taxes were very high, to supply the armies which defended the weakened frontiers. Vast sums of money were spent in the increasingly luxurious imperial court, which reached unparalleled degrees of splendour under Constantine the Great (under whom Christianity became the official religion of Rome).

EMPERORS AND NOBLES

The Emperor of the late Roman Empire was no longer just the most important citizen; copying the gorgeous display and ceremony of Persia, the Emperor was treated almost as a living god. His high officials had elaborate titles, and even lowly imperial clerks regarded themselves as ranking far above ordinary people.

In the late Roman world, it seems, although almost everyone was a Roman citizen, the gap between rich and poor was getting wider. Peasants in many areas became serfs, legally tied to the land, under the power of rich lords.

CATASTROPHE IN THE WEST

This new Roman Empire lasted until about AD 400, when the western half began to crumble in the face of barbarian invasions. Then, in AD 410, the world was shocked when Goths plundered Rome itself. Thereafter, most of Roman Europe, and even Africa, was gradually conquered by German invaders, who set up kingdoms in the old Roman lands. Some of these kingdoms eventually became the states of modern Europe: for example, the kingdom of the Franks (France) and the kingdoms of the Saxons and Angles (England).

The last Roman Emperor in the West, Romulus Augustulus, was deposed in AD 476 by the German general Odoacer, who became ruler of Italy.

SURVIVAL IN THE EAST

It is often forgotten that the Eastern Roman Empire survived, and for a long time remained a powerful state. Its capital was at Constantinople, the ancient Byzantium, hence the modern name, the 'Byzantine Empire'. The Byzantines resisted Persian might until both were attacked by the new power of Islam, erupting from the Arabian desert in the AD 630s. After centuries of Roman rule, Egypt and Syria were lost, although Turkey and parts of Europe were held. The Byzantine Empire survived until 1453, when Constantinople fell to the Turks.

The Byzantine Emperor Justinian (who reigned AD 527-565) reconquered Italy for a while. This beautiful mosaic, showing him with soldiers and bishops, is from a church he built at Ravenna in northern Italy.

In AD 410 a German tribe called the Visigoths, shown here, captured Rome. They looted the city, but did not do as much damage as the people who sacked it again in AD 455, and whose name is still notorious: the Vandals.

KEY DATES AND GLOSSARY

We are fortunate that many books and artefacts from the Roman Empire survive today. This means we can be quite certain of the dates of significant events after about **300** BC.

BC

700s Origins of Rome

753 Legendary foundation date of Rome

509 Overthrow of the last king; establishment of the Republic

390 Plunder of Rome by the Gauls

340-285 Wars against the Etruscans, Samnites, and North Italian Gauls

264-241 First Punic War with Carthage

241-225 Rome seizes Sicily, Sardinia and Corsica

218-201 Second Punic War; Hannibal invades Italy. Romans invade Spain

200-125 Roman provinces established in Spain, Southern France, Greece, Macedon, Turkey and North Africa.

149-146 The Third Punic War and the destruction of Carthage

100-31 Civil wars between warlords

58-51 Julius Caesar conquers Gaul

49-45 Caesar becomes sole ruler

44 Caesar assassinated

42-30 Renewed civil wars; Caesar's heir Octavian finally defeats Mark Antony. Egypt is made a province

27 Reign of Octavian (now called Augustus), first Emperor. End of the Republic, start of new imperial period

AD

14 Death of Augustus

37-41 Reign of Gaius (Caligula)

41-54 Reign of Claudius; conquest of Britain (begun 43)

54-68 Reign of Nero; great fire at Rome (64)

68-69 Civil wars

69-96 Reign of the Flavian dynasty, Vespasian and his sons

99-117 Reign of Trajan; conquest of Dacia, wars with Parthia

117-138 Reign of Hadrian

193-197 Civil wars

197-211 Reign of Septimius Severus

230-284 Chaos in the Empire: wars with Persia and Germans, and civil wars

284-305 Reign of Diocletian; peace, and reorganization of the Empire.

306-337 Reign of Constantine, the first Christian Emperor; foundation of Constantinople (330)

395 Empire divided into East and West

406-407 Breaching of the Rhine frontier: Germans overrun Gaul

406-476 Collapse of the Western Empire: Eastern Empire little affected

410 Visigoths capture Rome

476 Last Western Emperor, Romulus Augustulus, deposed

533-554 Eastern Emperor Justinian reconquers Italy and North Africa

634-642 Eastern (Byzantine) Empire loses Egypt and Syria to the armies of Islam

1453 Fall of Constantinople to the Turks; end of the Byzantine Empire

Glossary

amphitheatre: the arena invented for gladiators and animal fights

centurion: army officer in charge of a 'century' of 80 men

citizen: a free person with rights and privileges in his or her own city, or (if a Roman citizen) from Rome itself

Dacia: ancient state conquered by the Emperor Trajan in AD 113

equestrians: rich citizens, ranking below senators, who did many jobs in the army and civil service

genius: guardian spirit of a man (women were protected by a *Juno*)

governor: a Roman, usually a senator, in charge of a province (usually conquered land)

Latin: the language of the Roman city area, later spoken all over the Western Empire

legionary: a soldier in a 'legion', consisting of 5,500 Roman citizens

magistrate: someone holding elected office in Rome or another city, as judge, mayor, treasurer, etc

Parthian Empire: a powerful neighbour, on Rome's Eastern frontier, covering roughly modern Iraq and Iran

Pompeii: a minor Italian town buried by a volcanic eruption in AD 79

province: the land under a governor's care, or a magistrate's area of responsibility

relief: scenes and figures carved into the surface of a stone

sarcophagus: a stone coffin, often of marble and beautifully carved in 'relief'

senator\senate: at Rome, ex-magistrates became senators. Together, as the senate, they made laws

Quotations

Pliny (AD 61-114) was a writer whose *Letters* covered various subjects of concern to his contemporaries. Cicero (106-43 BC) was a statesman and orator who published his speeches and essays. The philosopher and writer Seneca (4 BC - AD 65) became tutor to the young Nero. The Greek writer Lucian (AD 117-180) made his fortune reciting show speeches whilst travelling the Empire, then devoted himself to philosophy. The books of the historian Appian (second century AD) were written during the reigns of the soldier-emperors Trajan, Hadrian and Marcus Aurelius.

INDEX

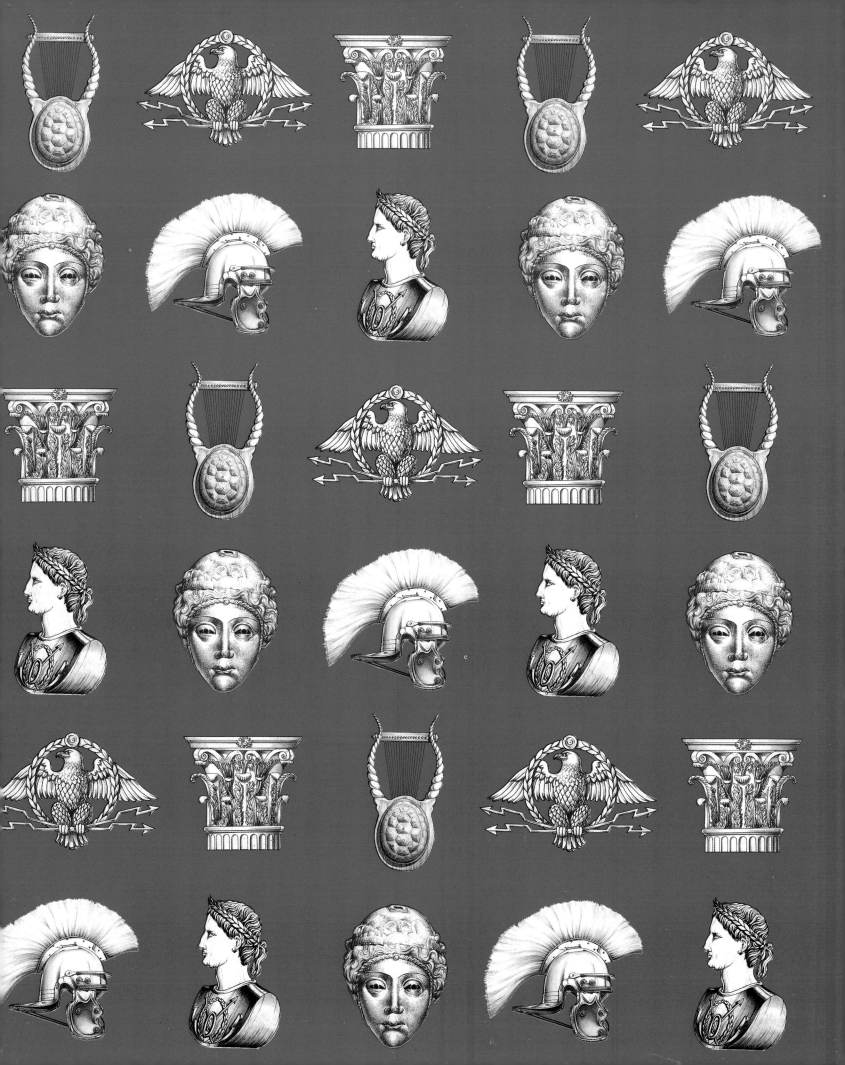